HIRING

Made Easy

WARNER MEMORIAL LIBRARY
EASTERN COLLEGE
ST. DAVIDS, PA. 19087

Jan Bailey

VGM Career Horizons

NTC/Contemporary Publishing Group

9-10-99

Library of Congress Cataloging-in-Publication Data

Jan Bailey.
    Hiring made easy / Jan Bailey.
       p.   cm. — (Made easy)
    ISBN 0-8442-6050-9
    1. Employee selection.   I. Title.   II. Series: Made easy
(Lincolnwood, Ill.)
    HF5549.5.S38M38   1998
    658.3' 112—dc21   98-33527
                                        CIP

HF 5549.5 .S38 B35 1999
Bailey, Jan.
Hiring made easy

Cover photograph copyright © SuperStock, Inc.
Cover design by Amy Ng
Interior design by City Desktop Productions, Inc.

Published by VGM Career Horizons
A division of NTC/Contemporary Publishing Group, Inc.
4255 West Touhy Avenue, Lincolnwood (Chicago), Illinois 60646-1975 U.S.A.
Copyright © 1999 by NTC/Contemporary Publishing Group, Inc.
All rights reserved. No part of this book may be reproduced, stored in a retrieval system, or
transmitted in any form or by any means, electronic, mechanical, photocopying, recording, or
otherwise, without the prior permission of NTC/Contemporary Publishing Group, Inc.
Printed in the United States of America
International Standard Book Number: 0-8442-6050-9

98 99 00 01 02 03 VP 20 19 18 17 16 15 14 13 12 11 10 9 8 7 6 5 4 3 2 1

HIRING

Made Easy

For Angela

who has taught me much of loyalty and friendship
and whose strength and wisdom is constant inspiration

Contents

Introduction

These are dynamic and challenging times for us all as individuals and as people in the business community. There is an interesting mix these days—big business is trying to streamline and become more competitive in an increasingly global economy and small business is growing at a rapid rate as people flex their entrepreneurial muscles. As a result, there is considerable transition in the business community and people are having to adapt to the changes.

Individuals, especially those in their own businesses, are taking on more tasks and becoming the ultimate business generalists, the masters of all trades. As a result of this, you may find yourself currently in the hiring seat with no idea how to start the engine.

Hiring Made Easy is just the coach you need. From deciding what it is your company needs, to writing an advertisement and interviewing potential employees, *Hiring Made Easy* helps you chart what may be unfamiliar territory.

If you've hired employees before, you will learn things to improve your technique and help you make excellent employee choices. If you have never hired an employee before, well, you'll learn everything you need to know.

So, a new day, a new challenge, a new experience . . . let's do it, and hey . . . let's have some fun out there!

 All glory comes from daring to begin.

Anonymous

Special Features

Special features throughout the book will help you pick out key points and help make the sometimes challenging task of hiring someone smooth and painless.

 Notes clarify text with concise explanations.

 Helpful Hints provide ideas and suggestions to improve your hiring techniques.

 Recruiting Resources provide insights into hiring, helping you understand the whys and the wherefores.

 Special Thoughts provide inspiration and motivation.

There's a void in your organization—let's get out there and fill it!

Chapter 1

In the Know

Our plans miscarry because they have no aim. When a man does not know what harbor he is making for, no wind is the right wind.

Seneca

The world of business—all business—is evolving at an alarming rate. It doesn't seem to matter if you manage a multibillion-dollar international corporation, a used auto parts yard, or a neighborhood cafe—your business, and what you do to stay in business, is changing.

Why?

As consumers, we want more; technology has enabled us to have and get more, and therefore we expect more.

What?

We want more. Like it or not, we have become a people and a society enamored with material wealth. We are perpetually slaving at one or two jobs, perhaps jobs we don't even like, in order to keep up with the Joneses. Somewhere in the course of history the rules changed and the "stuff" we had became synonymous with the happiness we enjoyed; more stuff, more happiness.

Now, as a direct result of this quest for material and monetary wealth, it seems time has virtually speeded up. Suddenly there is more to accomplish in a day: more work, more chores, more living. Fortunately, technology has enabled us to do and get more.

With the social desire and demand for increased material wealth, the pace of life and business has increased, quickly eating up the hours in a day. People are working longer hours at more than one job, perhaps running a small business from home, in addition to trying to spend quality time raising a family, and technology is right there keeping pace with it all.

Try to think of people in your life right now who don't complain about how little time and money they have. Are the people around you always tired and desperately wanting a vacation? These are all symptoms of the same problem. Do you fit in this category at work and/or at home?

More and more homes have personal computers, those computers are linked to the Internet, and when people leave home or travel they have a trusty laptop computer. We are constantly connected to the office with voice mail, E-mail, fax machines, cellular phones, and pagers. We can stay in touch with whatever and whomever we deem important: home, office, investment broker, banker, or baby-sitter, and once people have that convenience, few are willing to give it up.

So how does this affect you as a business owner or manager?

We expect more. As consumers in general, as customers of your business, and even as employees, people are more critical, more demanding, and definitely unwilling to wait for products or for services. Time and technology have made impatient consumers of us all. As a result, it is important that your business be prepared to greet this demanding, impatient new customer with speed, efficiency, and the latest in service technology. Ultimately, every business today must be concerned about customer service. Granted, some more than others, but every business has some kind of supplier and some kind of end user who is expecting more for their money and more for their time.

Never mistake motion for action.

Ernest Hemingway

We are surrounded by a consumer-driven, highly competitive marketplace, and as an employer in any sized company you must be conscious of the changes in the market and changes in customer habits. We are bigger consumers and spenders than we have ever been as a society, but we are also smarter shoppers, sometimes downright frugal, and we are forthright with our opinions of your company, good or bad. We are willing and able to shop around quickly for competitive products. We are suspicious of deals that look too good, too much "fine print" and slick salespeople, and if we are unhappy with a product or service, we are more than willing to speak out and demand better service and treatment. Even with all this in mind, today's consumer is still money conscious, concerned about value for the dollar, and always shops for a bargain—ultimately, a challenging person to please.

 You've heard the adage that if people are pleased with something, a service or product, they may tell one person they know. If they are unhappy with a service or product, they will tell everyone, even people they don't know!

Now, although all of this is very interesting, what exactly does it have to do with the fact that you need to hire someone for your business?

 Never try to teach a pig to sing; it wastes your time and it annoys the pig.

Paul Dickson

Well, it's all about supply and demand and vision. We've already decided that no matter what business you are in you have some kind of customer to please. That customer may not be "Joe Average," the consumer off the street who walks into your store and buys something, it may be another business, an export company, or a service which, in turn, deals directly with the public.

Whomever you sell your services to, they are your customers, and as customers, they want more from your product, from your after-sale service, and therefore from your staff.

Take a moment to consider who your customers are and what they value in your organization. What kind of employee would best suit their needs?

You can see where this is going. With this in mind, you must hire individuals who not only are skilled in whatever technology your company uses, good team players, current with the developments in your industry, and in line with your company mission, they must also be employees who ultimately work with the customer in mind. Service, service, service!

Particularly in today's increasingly competitive small businesses, employees must be skilled generalists, able to move smoothly and skillfully from one department to another, filling in where necessary and doing it comfortably.

A generalist is a term for an employee with a good overall "general" set of skills as opposed to someone who is a specialist—skilled and able to function well in only one particular field.

Additionally, as an employer, you must know where your organization is currently in the market, where you want to be in the future, how you plan to get there, and what kind of people will fit with your vision of that journey. Again, small business is increasingly competitive and companies are having to cut costs where possible to keep up, and that often translates into fewer employees doing a broader scope of tasks. Those employees you do hire must fit well with the rest of your team and must have a similar view of the future of the company in order to help it expand and stay focused.

The more aligned your employees' vision is with yours, the more likely they are to be long-term employees.

Only with *all* these things in mind can you make an appropriate, insightful, responsible, and ultimately successful decision about the kind of individual who will best suit your company. Indeed, you must consider what niche you want that individual to fill today, one year from now, and five years from now. Your company is constantly evolving, growing and changing with a dynamic consumer-driven market, and you need an individual who can match that dynamic and be a productive member of your team. So, before you can even begin to look for that kind of person, you must know exactly what your organization needs.

If you don't know where you are going, you will probably end up somewhere else.

Laurence J. Peter

Needs Analysis

This is important! A needs analysis is, for the most part, self-explanatory and quite possibly the most important thing you will do in the process of hiring someone for your business. It is the foundation for all things to follow and will determine everything from where you need to advertise to fill your position, to how the job will change in the next one, two, or five years. Simply put, "needs analysis" is a human resources term for you, as an employer, deciding what exactly your organization is looking for in an employee.

From what type of person would work best with the team and supervisor already in place, to the technical skills necessary to excel in the position, a needs analysis defines *exactly* what your organization requires from the "ideal" or "dream" candidate. Additionally, a comprehensive needs analysis assesses the environment of your company, your plans for expanding or streamlining, your projected future, and how a new employee can best complement all those areas.

Begin this process by looking at the mandate or mission statement of your organization. This will help you refocus and get you thinking globally (encompassing all aspects of the company) and about hiring for your future.

Granted, it sounds complicated at the outset, but you will find the needs analysis helpful with your business in general as well as your hiring process. Indeed, if you hope this will be a successful hiring venture, and one you will not have to repeat several times over, be prepared to spend some quality time defining the overall needs of your organization and the specific needs of the position you are filling.

All too often when it comes down to the interviewing and hiring stage of this time-consuming process, employers find their knowledge of the position and environment lacking and often hire someone they "like" who may not be the best-suited candidate for the job. Certainly this is not to say you shouldn't hire someone you like, but it is too easy to get caught up with personal chemistry and feelings and over-look the real requirements of your company. It's great if you happen to have fly fishing in common with your new employee and you both frequent the same freshwater streams, but if you allow yourself to get caught up in that commonality and forget the real needs of your company team, you may quickly find yourself wishing for less fishing and more effective work.

Plan to do a thorough needs analysis for your company well before you begin the hiring process. It will save you time, money, and frustration in the long run.

Sadly, there are no shortcuts in deciding what exactly it is you want and require from a new employee. There are, however, some things you may want to consider to make the process as successful as possible.

What?

Whether you are personally hiring the individual who will fill this position, or you are enlisting the assistance of a professional agency or recruiter, you, as the employer, must know the environment you are hiring for.

Even if you are paying an agency to hire for you, you are still the main source of information with respect to the position. Either way, you must be familiar with your needs.

Ask yourself:

1. *What kind of person would complement the skills of the team already in place?* Is the team lacking in certain areas, and what type of individual would be able to pick up the slack?

Meet with the person who would supervise the new employee and some of the people who would work closely with him or her. Get their input and suggestions on what is needed and what would best benefit the team.

2. *Is there new technology infiltrating the industry or environment with which this individual must be familiar?* Is the office fast becoming computerized, and is it necessary for the individual you hire to be completely computer literate?

You must decide ahead of time how much time, energy, and money you are willing to devote to initially training your new employee.

3. *What type of personality is the supervisor of this position, and what style of management does he or she use?* The supervisor must work closely with the new employee. He or she should be involved in some capacity in the hiring process to ensure there will be a productive and positive working relationship.

4. *How large, small, or closely knit is the current team?* Often the people working directly in the department, not management, will have a better idea of what type of person would best complement the team already in place. They may, in fact, have very strong opinions about what is essential.

5. *Is this a long-term, growth position or simply a contract position that will be around for only a year or so?* Determining how long the position will be active will dictate how skilled and compatible with your team the new employee must be.

 Contract or term positions often evolve into full-time employment. Don't be too lenient with a contract employee's "fit" thinking he or she will not be around long.

6. *What kind of person will "fit" with the team in place and the mandate or long-term vision of the company?* Hiring and training an appropriate employee is an expensive and time-consuming process. You want to be as sure as possible the individual you hire is one who will fit well enough to grow with your team and your organization.

7. *Do your clients and customers have specific needs and demands that would be best supplied by a certain type of individual?* Although you can't hire with only the customers in mind, it certainly helps in the long run to consider what type of person they respond well to and, frankly, what kind of person they like.

Since you may have to compromise, consider your priorities: all the technical skills and education to the letter, or someone whose personality and attitude fit extremely well with the rest of the team but who would need to learn some of the technical end.

Keeping all these things in mind will help you get a firm grasp of your company, its direction, its needs for the future, and most important, the kind of employee who will move and grow effectively along with your organization. Although it may seem ridiculous, trivial, or redundant to evaluate and reassess your own company, you may be surprised by what you learn.

Even if the position you are hiring for is not your department, familiarize yourself thoroughly with it. Not only will it give you a solid grasp of what the department needs, it will make you much more effective in the interview stage.

Oftentimes we get caught up in the day-to-day business of things and forget to step back and chart where it is we initially planned to go. A needs analysis can nicely help you regroup and redefine what it is you want from your company and the team that helps you run it (not to mention, help you find a suitable employee, of course!).

A good manager is a man who isn't worried about his own career but rather the careers of those who work for him. My advice: Don't worry about yourself. Take care of those who work for you and you'll float to greatness on their achievements.

H. S. M. Burns
President, Shell Oil Company

Let's take a minute to regroup. Check your progress against the following checklist. You have

- evaluated your organization's current position in the market and know where you want your company to be in one, two, five years

- decided you require an additional employee to assist you in your growth

- spoken to the position supervisor to determine what he or she feels is essential to the position

- discussed the position with those who will be peers of the new employee, discovered their strengths and weaknesses, and decided how a new person would best complement them

- surveyed customers and stakeholders of your company to assess what qualities they think are necessary in a successful candidate

- closely considered what role and responsibilities a new employee would take on to help take your company in the direction you want it to go

If you have considered all these things your needs analysis is moving along quite nicely: just remember at this point to continue to think globally. No, not globally with respect to world marketplace, but globally with respect to your company. You must continue to think of this position and the individual who will fill it in terms of how they will affect the entire company, not simply one isolated position.

Particularly in small businesses today, every person in your employ must be a hardworking, integral part of your organization to ensure it runs well and profitably. Also, when you hire successfully, your new employee will hopefully stay with you for some time. With that in mind, your needs analysis must take into consideration additional training, financial compensation, and job expansion for this person within the company. Good grief, all of this to consider! And you thought you were just going to put an ad in the paper!

A man can stand almost anything except a succession of ordinary days.

Goethe

To this point we have been working under the assumption that this is a new position which needs to be filled in your organization. There is, of course, the distinct possibility that someone is simply leaving the company (for any number of reasons), and you have to fill the resulting vacancy. It is still essential that you, or whomever is responsible for hiring, become familiar with the position and the needs of the team.

Why?

- The employee who is leaving may have been there a considerable length of time, and you may not be familiar with the position.

- The company itself may have changed considerably during the person's employ.

- The company may currently be growing or undergoing direction changes, and the position itself may need to be redefined.

- Other individuals may have been hired whose job descriptions overlap or encompass this position, making it obsolete.

Indeed, all of these things need to be considered, but you may gain some welcome assistance from the person who is leaving the position by conducting an exit interview.

Exit Interview

An exit interview, if you have the opportunity to do one, is a blessing when it comes to an effective needs analysis. Speaking with an employee who is "exiting" a position amicably gives you excellent means to learn about the position and what type of person would best fill it.

Now, once again, provided the individual is leaving your company on favorable terms, set aside some time to discuss the job with him or her. The past incumbent can be a wealth of information for you, and because he or she is leaving the company you can probably expect quite honest and candid responses. So, steal him or her away in a private meeting for an hour or so and ask away.

 It is probably to your advantage to interview the past incumbent privately, not in the presence of his or her direct supervisor or peers.

You might like to know

- What are the key things you do in your job?

- What kind of person is your supervisor?

- What kind of personality do you think would work best with your supervisor?

- What are the challenges of your job?

- What are the mundane or routine aspects of the position?

- If you could change your job in any way, how would you?

- What are your thoughts on the company itself?

- Is it a good organization to work for or not?

- How would you change the company if you could?

- What training do you feel would have benefited you and made you more effective in your position?

- If you had the opportunity to hire for this position to replace yourself, what would you look for in a candidate? Why?

You get the idea.

Those who cannot remember the past are condemned to repeat it.

Santayana

This is a marvelous chance for you to get the inside information on the position and, as a result, to be able to troubleshoot before hiring someone new. You may decide the department needs to be reshuffled somewhat, you may decide the responsibilities of the position need to change, or you may decide the position is completely unnecessary. Whatever you decide, take full advantage, if you can, of the exit interview.

So, by now you should have a fairly complete picture in your mind of the type of person you need to fill the vacancy in your company. Certainly everyone you speak with and ask for input from will have different priorities regarding what qualities are most important in your new employee. Ultimately, however, as the employer, you must decide who will have final say regarding who to hire.

Do not feel that because you are the employer you must hire this individual. You may choose to contract the hiring out, or you may choose to have the people who will work directly with this person do the hiring. It's your choice.

With the needs analysis groundwork virtually complete you have firsthand knowledge of what is required of your soon-to-be new team member. With all this in mind, the goals and the ideals, now is a good time to write a comprehensive job description.

Job Description

As you begin to logically write down what this new or revised position will entail, keep one thing in mind: you are, at this moment, probably the only person who knows exactly what the position is. You have done the research, you have done the team interviews, you have done the customer surveys—you are the person in the know.

What is the point?

Well, the point is that it is a perfectly natural human tendency to assume that because you are aware of something, everyone close to you is as well. Or, conversely, because you know, no one else really needs to. Well, it doesn't work that way in this case. The more people you can make aware of this (and every) job description, the better.

Running any kind of business is an absurd amount of work, and the easier your job is, the better. So . . . write down job descriptions, make people aware of them, and use them.

Anyone can do any amount of work, provided it isn't the work he is supposed to be doing.

Robert Benchley

OK, that short and painless little lecture is over. Now you can focus on the task at hand, which is composing a written job description encompassing all you have learned and having it evaluated by those most closely connected to the position.

Your initial draft of the job description will probably be ridiculously long and detailed. Do not despair, it will naturally come into to focus as you review it again and again.

The job description you originally compose will, no doubt, evolve as the new employee you selected becomes comfortable with the company and the position. In the beginning, however, the written job description should encompass the scope of the position.

What?

The scope of the position is the position in its entirety, the whole shebang, the complete deal, from beginning to end, from the outset, through the proposed evolutionary stages to the peak of the position. Good grief, it sounds impossible before you even begin! Fear not . . . this written explanation of the scope of the position will change a certain amount, but it is essential for you and for the new employee to have a foundation from which to begin. There is nothing more frustrating for someone you hire than floundering around trying to become familiar with a new company, the people who work there, and a new position that has a name, but seemingly no specific responsibilities. It can even be frustrating to you, too.

If you have an old job description and are fortunate enough to do an exit interview, be sure to get input from the former employee as to how valid and accurate that description was.

As the word "scope" implies, you should have some idea where the responsibilities of this position begin in your organization and where, as your company strives toward its goals, they will end. Once again, this demands that you as an employer have a good solid idea where your company is headed in the future, and how you plan to have your staff grow and change along with you.

Do not panic. Remember, this is an outline, and as with any good plan, it will change as your company changes.

It is a bad plan that admits of no modification.

Pubilius Syrus

There are a number of things to consider as you work toward developing a functioning job description, and certainly only you know the specifics of your particular company and its needs.

Here is some food for thought:

- Are you planning to expand your company, or is it currently as big as you hoped it would be?

- If your company does expand, how will this position change?

- Is there room for the employee to move within the organization: laterally or upwardly? Will you encourage or discourage this?

- Will the new employee be expected to continually upgrade his or her skills and education? Are you prepared to pay for it?

- Will the new employee be supervising other employees now and/or in the future?

- Is there a possibility that you may open businesses in other locations or move your business? How will you keep your employees with you?

- What range of salary are you willing to pay?

- Does your company offer some type of benefit or profit-sharing plan? Will you in the future?

If the company profits, the employees profit—a philosophy that makes for a healthy, happy, and productive work environment.

Obviously you cannot plan for every circumstance that may occur in or to your company. For example, you may sell, merge with another similar or completely different organization, or business may suddenly take a turn for the better or worse. By taking the time to think about some of the possibilities, though, you increase the likelihood that your new employee will be happy and successful in his or her new position.

Keep in mind while you compose this job description that this must be a mutually beneficial relationship for it to work out well and for the long term. What does this mean?

Well, for an employee to be productive, to remain productive, to grow with the company, to offer insight, ideas, and initiative to the position, he or she must be happy. Now happy does not necessarily only mean money. Certainly adequate remuneration is essential, but that isn't the only factor.

- A person must feel as though he or she is an important component in the company.

- The job must be sufficiently challenging to keep the employee stimulated and interested.

- There must be a feeling that the employee is an important factor in the growth and direction of the company, not simply another spoke in the wheel.

- It is important that every individual in an organization feel as though he or she matters to the team—his or her opinions, ideas, and work.

 These statements all refer to the concept of empowerment: ensuring your employees feel as though they are integral parts of your organization from decision making to production.

Consider all these things at the outset of the hiring procedure. What are you hoping to gain from this new employee-employer relationship, and what are you prepared to give?

 His job must not only feed his body; it must sustain his spirit.

Daniel Bell

Granted, this seems like an awful lot of work before you've even begun to advertise the position or interview potential candidates. It will be worth it in the long run—really. Your well-thought-out, comprehensive job description will give the new employee somewhere to begin in his or her new job in times when there is no one available to direct him or her personally, it will help other employees understand how the addition of this new person will affect their positions, and, most importantly, it will give you, the employer, a basis on which to evaluate the individual's performance.

 You will also find your newly created job description very helpful when writing the advertisement for the position.

Chapter 2

From Paper to People

 The trouble with unemployment is that the minute you wake up in the morning you're on the job.

Slappy White

Here we are, phase two. What may have seemed like endless groundwork doing a needs analysis is now completed and you have a solid grasp of your organization, its goals, and your staffing needs.

Now what?!

Well, once again, it's time to consider your options and what best meets your company's needs. You may now choose to obtain the services of a headhunter, executive search firm, or recruiting agency to do your staffing, or you may complete the hiring process yourself.

Certainly there are benefits to both, depending on your time frame, needs, and financial position. Let's start with a few definitions and some comparisons just to make sure everyone is up to speed.

Headhunters and Executive Search Firms

These are professional agencies designed specifically to locate, interview, and screen potential candidates for companies. They make it their business to know who are the up-and-coming executives in a number of fields. They are skilled recruiters and make it their business to be familiar with everything from the latest in effective hiring practices to competitive industry salaries.

It's a great idea to do an information-gathering interview with a headhunter to find out exactly what they do and to get some insight into the recruiting process.

Since headhunters make it their business to be in the know and on the cutting edge of what is happening in their specialty industry, individuals looking for work will also enlist their assistance and routinely check in with them to discuss movement in the corporate world. Whether these individuals are currently unemployed, working on a specific contract, or employed full time, the headhunter will know what kind of offer would help them consider a move to your company. As a result, by employing the services of a headhunter, you may have access to skilled individuals who would consider a move to a different organization, but who are not actively circulating their resumes.

Certainly there are headhunters and executive search firms that have particular specialties. Shop around till you find one appropriate for your needs.

Put simply, think of this as a kind of dating service where the headhunter or executive search firm is the matchmaker looking for the perfect fit between company and individual!

Pros

1. These services nicely take the majority of the responsibility of hiring off your hands. They will take a job description from you (OK, you do still have to create one!), ask you what specific qualities you are looking for in an employee and what your fundamental needs are (you are also required to know those!), and then they will do the rest. In the end, you will have five, or ten if you wish, of the top candidates to interview on your own schedule.

2. They will also assist you in the interview process if you choose. This can indeed be a blessing if you have not done a lot of hiring for your company. Good interviewing is a learned skill and one that is essential to discovering the best-suited employee for your company.

 Don't be embarrassed to admit interviewing is not your forte. No one is great at everything!

3. Additionally, the search firm will continue to look for a suitable candidate until one is found who meets your needs.

Cons

1. It is virtually impossible for an outside agency to come into your organization and in a few short meetings *know* your company. As a result, it is challenging (not impossible) for them to find the perfect-fit employee. Unfortunately, no one can know your company as well as you do, from team dynamics to customer quirks, so you must take that into consideration if you choose to enlist the services of one of these agencies.

If every man stuck to his talent the
cows would be well tended.

J. P. DeFlorian

2. The cost for an executive search can cost in the neighborhood of
$20,000. Now granted, if you add up all the time and energy you and
the rest of the management interview team might spend recruiting
and hiring a new staff member, you may very well come close to that
figure. Only you can decide if it is worth it to you to pay out that
kind of fee, in one lump sum, for a service.

 **Both headhunters and executive
search firms deal almost exclusively
with "suits," or upper management
and executive positions. Please see
recruiting agencies for other
positions!**

 **ecruiting Agencies**

A recruiting agency by definition is virtually the same thing as an
executive search firm, without the *executive* part. A recruiting agency
will assist you with your staffing needs when you are not in the market for
management. The services of every type of employee from administrative
assistant to day laborer may be contracted or hired through an agency.

 **As with the headhunter, recruiting
agencies have specialties. For
example, a particular agency may
deal exclusively with people skilled
with computers, or with cleaning
services, or gardening.**

Pros

1. Once again, it is quite convenient to hand your hiring woes over to an agency with experience and expertise.

2. The staff of the recruiting agency will assist you from beginning to end. Starting with your needs analysis, they will then advertise, screen, and even help you interview the top five (or as many as you choose) candidates if you wish.

3. Often recruiting agencies, like headhunters, have a roster of individuals whom they have already met and prescreened (prescreening simply means the individuals are preinterviewed to determine skill and motivation level, etc.). This may help speed up the process for you.

 It may be in your best interest to have an ad run for the position unless the agency has someone in mind who would be absolutely perfect. With respect to staffing, more choices are often preferable to fewer choices.

Cons

1. As with executive search firms, you can never be certain a recruiting agency knows exactly what the goals, mission, and mandate of your organization are. You simply must go on the hope that they can see the vision of your company and can use that insight to find the ideal candidate.

2. As always, there is a cost involved.

Again, once you take into account the time you would spend in all aspects of recruiting, you may find the agency fee nominal.

Now, remember, even if you choose to contract the services of one of these agencies, you will still have some work to do. You cannot expect someone with no prior knowledge of your company to come in and immediately assess your organization without assistance and make snap decisions on what type of individual is appropriate for your company. You will still have to do a comprehensive needs analysis and interview with the agency to give the recruiters somewhere to begin. With that in mind, you may choose to complete the hiring process on your own.

Completing the Hiring Process on Your Own

If this is the decision you make, we are right back to where we left off: you have completed your needs analysis and composed a comprehensive job description (that may still be in a state of evolution, which is fine), and it is time to write an advertisement to seek out the optimal employee.

 There is something in every person's character that cannot be broken—the bony structure of his character. Wanting to change it is the same as teaching a sheep to retrieve.

George C. Lichtenberg

Now, just a little aside before we get right down to the business of composing an ad: consider the possibility that you may not even need to advertise. In fact, while you are doing the preparation work to hire someone, the needs analysis, the written job description, etc., you would be wise to use this time to do a little networking on behalf of your company. Be sure to ask the people who work with you, for you, and in the same industry as you if they are aware of qualified people looking for work.

If you have ever been on the other side of this equation looking for employment it is the same process— with a bit of a twist!

It is not all that unusual for companies looking for skilled employees to keep an eye on the competition who may be downsizing their organizations. If one company is downsizing or restructuring in some manner and another looking to hire someone, it only makes sense that there be an exchange of information and manpower. You should always make it your business to be aware of what the competition is doing. However, when you are looking to hire, you should go out of your way to know the comings and goings of your industry.

Make it a practice in your everyday working to be open to people seeking information about your company— students doing information-gathering interviews or requesting work practicum experience, or simply people wanting to drop off unsolicited resumes. By making time for these various individuals (within reason, of course) you may find your-self with a stockpile of potential employees.

So, if you are well connected in your industry and have made it an ongoing practice to stay on top of "who's who," you may be lucky enough to not need to advertise. Certainly if you asked people looking for work, they would tell you it is extremely frustrating when employers network for employees and don't advertise. It is, however, to your advantage to be able to do so.

How can you begin to build your network?

By asking

- your employees if they know of people who are interested and appropriately skilled for your position

- your customers if they know of quality people who are looking for work

- your suppliers if they know people in a related industry who may be interested in a change in company

- the competition if they are shuffling their organization at all

- your contemporaries if they have someone in their network who is looking for employment

By beginning to network in this way, you may be lucky enough to find someone appropriate for your organization, meaning you effectively bypass the time-consuming and costly process of advertising and screening potentially hundreds of resumes.

There is no such thing as a problem
without a gift for you in its hands.

R. Bach

Of course, barring the small blessing that you do, in fact, find someone through your networking channels who knows someone who knows someone—you get the idea—whom you hire without even having to advertise, you will have to write an advertisement for your position.

 riting Your Ad

There are a few things to consider when composing your ad. You must think of where it will run and for how long. Keeping cost in mind (which every business does), you will also need to create the most specific ad possible in the least amount of newspaper or advertising space (obviously newspapers and magazines charge you by the amount of space you use in the publication).

You are probably asking yourself, "But don't I want a general advertisement to attract the most people possible so I can have a nice selection of people to choose from?"

In a word—no!

 Browse through the career section of your local newspaper and in the classified ads for a couple of weeks. You will quickly learn which are well written and effective ads and which are not. Don't be afraid to steal some ideas!

Unless you are looking for extremely technical, cutting-edge, finely detailed qualifications (advanced computer skills come to mind), you will probably receive more than enough resumes. Granted there will be many of them that are not even remotely close to what you are looking for in an employee, but hopefully those will be the minority. Therefore, the more specific an ad you can write, the more candidates it will weed out for you right off the top.

The first line or two of your advertisement will be a preamble to your company. This should cover things such as

- who your company is
- what your company does
- your vision for the future of the organization
- what you're looking for in an employee

The next one or two lines gives a description of the position, which should be easy since you have your well-researched job description to refer to!

You should be starting to see the sequence and evolution of this process—and the benefit of doing it in stages.

Next, add to the advertisement what specific requirements the successful candidate must have. For example, you may expect the person to have a particular degree or certification.

 In the job description, it is a good idea to mention if the position is temporary, contract, or part time; requires extensive travel; or has the possibility of relocation at a later date. These are the kinds of things that will assist those reading the ad in eliminating themselves from the competition. There is no point in having people apply, subsequently interviewing and wanting to hire them only to have them decline the position because they were not aware they would have to travel around the country. Save yourself the time, effort, and anxiety and be as specific as possible.

Now, in one line or less, add any assets that you would consider a definite bonus. For example, experience dealing specifically with a nonprofit organization, experience working with visually impaired children, specialized computer knowledge—you get the idea. Think of this as your employee wish list—"the ideal candidate would have . . ."

 Be absolutely certain to keep your advertisement gender neutral! This means you are advertising your position to anyone who is interested—male or female and of any ethnic origin.

Finally, include the details of how to apply for the position. This is the space to tell people what you want them to do with their resume and/or application form. Would you like them to drop them off at the office, mail them to a post office box, or fax them to you?

The nice thing about faxed resumes is there are no envelopes to deal with, no staples or paper clips, and you don't have to date stamp them—the fax machine does it for you.

Additionally, add points such as "no phone calls, please" (if you do not include this you are guaranteed to receive countless phone calls), the name of the person to address cover letters to, and any other details of the application process you would like followed.

Of course you may want to have people call in to give you an indication of interest in the position and as another form of prescreening and gleaning a first impression.

As the closing note, you may wish to thank everyone for applying and mention that only those selected for an interview will be contacted. This saves you from making endless phone calls or sending out form letters thanking candidates and informing them the position has been filled.

Why do you even need to do this?

Well, to begin with, as a courtesy to those who were interested and made the effort to apply to your company.

Common sense is genius dressed in its working clothes.

Ralph Waldo Emerson

Second, if you do not inform people that the position has been filled, they will assume the competition is ongoing. This means people will continue to call and/or drop by to "see how the hiring process is progressing." Overall, it is in your best interest to make the details of the hiring time line and process public knowledge.

Hopefully, at this point, you have an advertisement for a position with your company! No doubt your first draft will be longer than you want and probably more than you can afford. Do not despair. Refer again to your job description and needs analysis and edit out what is unnecessary. Remember, you are trying to entice well-qualified, interested people to your company, not bore them with unimportant details.

Have several people read your advertisement and give you their impressions and ideas. If only you have been working on it, a new perspective is essential.

OK, your ad is complete. In a nutshell it has captured the broad scope of the company and the position, the key skills and abilities of the person best suited to fill that position, and the specific tasks of the job and the tools needed to perform them.

Now, take some time to seriously consider where the ad would be best placed.

What? Why?

Well, for example, if you are looking for someone for your customer-service department who is bilingual, consider running your advertisement in the local cultural magazine or posting it on billboards at the appropriate cultural center.

Or, if you are looking for someone with the very latest skills in a particular computer programming language, perhaps you should consider placing your ad in specific educational institutions that offer courses in what you require.

You get the idea. The point is, running an ad does not necessarily mean only placing it in the Saturday or Sunday employment section of the largest paper in town. You are looking for quality people, and you may have to be a bit creative to find them.

When writing ads, the shorter the headline the longer it stays in somebody's head.

Tom Allen

Add to this the financial consideration. You may be part of a small organization that cannot afford an ad in the career section of a large paper, and you therefore must be ingenious with where you run your ad and how you spend your money. By advertising in smaller, local, cultural, university, or college papers you still target a fairly large readership, yet odds are the cost to run your ad will be less. Compare that lower cost with the "no cost" involved in posting your advertisement on school billboards or in community centers.

Even if you do have the budget to run your ad in a large newspaper, it is still a good idea to target some of these specific venues.

Again, much of this comes down to budget and the kind of candidate you are looking for. Having, at this point, put considerable thought into what you are looking for in an employee, you should have a very good idea of what you need your ad to say and where you will want it posted.

As the Internet picks up users, it is also a location to be considered for running your ad, particularly if you are hiring technology-minded employees.

Despite all your efforts to compile a comprehensive advertisement, have it run in appropriate publications, and do some networking on your own all the while, statistics suggest you may still find a lack of quality applications.

Economics, Math, and Birth Control

Though it seems we still hear routinely about layoffs and downsizing, you may find yourself experiencing difficulty attracting the ideal, or even a suitable, candidate for your position. Particularly if your business is computer related or high-end technical in some way, you may be in for an extended search. What is going on?

From an employer's perspective, it is essential in the current business market to continually train employees and plan for future growth and direction of your organization.

Well, there are a number of factors contributing to what some human resource professionals are terming a staffing drought. Indeed, many companies are downsizing their staff, but there are less and less people in the workforce. How can that be? Simple math combined with economics and birth control gives us the answer!

What?

Simply put, the baby boomers are beginning to retire and leave the workforce, or at least cut back on their hours at work, and there are simply not enough skilled workers to pick up the slack. If you recall, the boomers are the postwar generation, born to a time of rebuilding economies and huge growth in virtually every industry.

 The baby boom was from 1946 through 1964.

This generation grew up in a work world of stability, full benefit packages, retirement plans—the full meal deal. So now, at the turn of the century, the first half of the boomers are thinking about retirement, or are retiring, and are therefore freeing up a lot of room in the business world, particularly in management positions. Certainly this seems like a good thing, more jobs for the people still working, until we consider the math and birth control aspect of things.

In the middle of difficulty lies opportunity.

Albert Einstein

This is going somewhere, really it is! The generation to follow the boomers was born in an economic time not quite so growth oriented and lucrative. Business markets had slowed down to a certain degree, and companies that had gone through huge growth spurts were leveling off. So, while the boomers' parents had no reason to think their job security was at risk and could therefore have large families (which is part of the reason for the baby boom phenomenon), the baby boomers themselves were not quite so certain of their economic future and therefore limited their family size.

The point?

Years ago, some 76 million baby boomers entered the workforce, creating jobs and companies. This was great. However, the generation following that boom is now coming into its own in the workforce, but there are only 50 or so million of them to do it. Obviously there are jobs around that simply cannot be filled. Economics, math, and birth control!

Luck is being ready for the chance.

J. Frank Dobie

Additionally, many of the individuals who were victims of downsizing took their generous severance packages and invested them in businesses of their own, thereby fueling the small business market—the source of the majority of employment opportunities today.

Add to that employers wanting increasingly diverse and skilled employees, and you have what may prove to be a challenging marketplace to hire in.

If you are looking for work and are skilled and flexible, this may be a great marketplace for you. If you are an employer in any sized business, well, it is a job-seeker's market.

All this adds up to some important points:

1. Be prepared to do some serious screening of applicants before you find those suitable to interview.
2. Be prepared to have your hiring endeavors take some time and effort.
3. Be prepared to do some innovative searching for employees.
4. Be prepared to compromise to a degree when you do hire.
5. Be prepared to do some training with your new employees.

Now is certainly the time to prepare for future staffing. Be sure to consider promoting and hiring from within. This means continually training and grooming your employees, but it is well worth it in the long run.

Well, as you read this, hopefully your ad has been running, the resumes are piling up, and you are at a loss as to what to do next!

Let the Screening Begin

Until your officially advertised closing date arrives, all you need to do with the resumes you receive is take them out of their envelopes or off the fax machine, date stamp them as to when you received them, and put them all in a nice pile.

If you wish, take a quick glance at each resume when you receive it, but don't make any judgments about it until you have all the resumes you are planning to accept in front of you.

Additionally, if a candidate drops off a resume in person, be sure to have whoever accepts the resume take note of his or her first impressions of that candidate. *Do not* write any personal comments directly on the resume. Use a sticky note or attach a separate piece of paper, but *never* write anything personal, be it good or bad, directly on someone's resume. Not only is this a human rights issue, but you never know when the candidate may come back and say, "Oops, I mistakenly gave you the original copy of my resume, can I have it back to make another copy?" That would be fine except for the fact that you've written on it in black felt pen, "seems nice enough, but ugly suit and bad haircut"! Remember, it is, after all, the applicant's resume, and he or she may ask to see it or have it back at any time.

OK, now that we're clear on that aspect of things . . . you still have the pile of resumes in front of you to deal with. This is going to take some time, so get yourself a glass of water, a comfortable chair, and your reading glasses.

 It's a good idea to do this all in one day so you stay in the same "groove." Double-check your choices the next day, but once you are in "resume frame of mind," try to stay there until the screening task is complete.

Refresh and Regroup

The first thing you should do before you even begin reading any of the resumes in front of you is quickly remind yourself of all the things you need and want in an employee. Refresh your memory and focus your priorities again by reading your needs analysis and the job description for the position. Now, let's do it.

The Three Screen

Read quickly, or skim, through each resume and divide them into three basic categories:

- This person looks like he or she has what I want in an employee.

- Maybe this person has what I want in an employee.

- This person definitely does not have what I want in an employee.

Remember, use your priority criteria to do this first division of resumes, whether it is education, experience, a combination of both, or whatever. Keep in mind, also, that this is a fairly quick read, and once you have done the initial "three screen," we'll call it, you will read the resumes in greater detail.

OK, you now have three distinct piles of resumes. Take the "no" pile and set it aside, which will help limit the choices, and concentrate on the two remaining. Depending on how many resumes you began this process with, you probably have twenty or so left that have at least piqued your interest. Now it gets serious! Get out your pen and prepare to read these twenty a little more closely. Circle things that you find interesting, things that impress you, or things that don't quite make sense to you, for whatever reason.

 Remember, all you are doing is circling and checking things off. Do not make notes on the resume, use a separate piece of paper.

The Long List

So, with all this new information you have discovered in your second, more detailed read of the resumes, you should be able to narrow the field even further. From twenty resumes, you are now hopefully down to ten. This group of ten is called your "long list," and they are the people who have made the first cut as the best candidates for your position.

Remember, ten is just a random number. You may have only five or six, but ideally you don't want to have to closely pick through too many more than ten.

From here on in the competition is, presumably, a little tougher, and you will have to read these ten resumes quite closely.

 Feel free to take a break at this point! Your water glass is probably empty!

As you read the ten resumes in front of you, look for specific things that you would like to question the candidate about. For example, there may be unexplained gaps in the resume or particular projects listed that you would like to know more about. Again, use a separate piece of paper and make notes as you go through.

Why?

Because the next stage of the process is calling all candidates.

Calling All Candidates

Calling? Yes, picking up the phone and calling.

Now these phone calls will not be overly long conversations, but they are very important. Here is your chance to speak with the candidates directly and ask them any of the questions that came up while you were screening their resume. For instance, you can ask a candidate about the gap in his resume between such and such dates, or when she will complete the computer course she is currently enrolled in, etc.

 The learned person is not the one who gives the right answer but the one who asks the right questions.

Claude Levi-Strauss

In addition to resume-specific questions, take this opportunity to ask the candidates more general questions that will give you some insight into their character:

- why they are applying for this position
- why they are leaving their current position
- what type of salary they expect

and so on.

But wait, before you begin calling these people, there are a few confidentiality or, if you prefer, courtesy issues which must be considered.

What?

Well, for instance, you don't know if these people have informed their current employers that they are applying for other employment. If you are calling them at work, be certain to ask them if they are able to speak freely with you or if there is a more appropriate time when you could call them back. It is in your best interest to have these people answer all your questions honestly and openly, so give them a fair opportunity to do so.

If you do not reach them when you call the first time, do not leave your name with whomever answers the phone. You do not want to make it awkward for them at their current position and have unnecessary questions being asked.

Do not leave a message even if you receive their voice mail. Again, you do not know if the voice mail is confidential, and it is no one's business but theirs that they are applying for other employment.

It is even a good idea to speak with the telephone operator or dial the code to have your number blocked from caller ID. With today's technology many companies know who is calling them before they even pick up the phone. Once again, this could create difficulties for the individual you are calling, especially if you happen to be the competition!

With all of these things in mind, go ahead—make the calls!

At the End of the Day

Goodness, you've had a busy day! OK, this whole process has probably taken you more than one day, especially combined with the phone calls you had to make. You no doubt learned some valuable information, however. Perhaps some of the candidates could not answer your questions, and others answered them much more completely than you could have hoped. Perhaps you found some individuals who wanted more money than your organization could possibly offer and others who exaggerated beyond belief when it came to their skills and experience. Whatever you found, it was no doubt interesting, and you should now be able to narrow the field to the top three to five candidates for your position.

 Remember, this is a suggested number of top candidates. Three would be ideal, but certainly no more than five candidates should be interviewed.

So, congratulations are in order! You took an intimidating stack of resumes and through perseverance and focus you have three candidates who are moving on to the interview portion of the hiring process! You deserve some praise because this is a time-consuming process that takes a lot of background work and patience, and you are doing very well.

Moving along . . . to more background work and organization that will also take much patience!

What?

Onward, to the interviews.

Chapter 3

Interviewing Insights

 Always be smarter than the people who hire you.

Lena Horne

There were times you weren't sure you would make it this far, but you did and now you need to schedule interviews. Once again, there are some decisions to make and some things to consider.

What?

Well, to begin with:

1. Who should be included in the interview process?

2. How many candidates will be interviewed?

3. How many interviews will candidates be required to pass through?

4. Where will the interviews be held?

5. Does it matter when you schedule the interviews?

As you can see, there are a few more things to consider than, "Gee, I guess we should get together sometime to chat about this new job." OK, it probably isn't that bad, but, no matter how casual, informal, laid back, or unstructured your organization is, there must be a certain amount of planning, forethought, and structure put into this process. All too often interviews begin as informal, get-to-know-you sessions with no apparent direction and end up not quite working out. Interviewers frequently have the notion that things will simply evolve in conversation, and information that must be exchanged will simply "come out" in the natural course of things. The end result of this strategy is that candidates often need to come back for a second or third interview because certain questions were not asked and answered, or key people who should have been included in the interview were not.

 Do not be afraid to do some research into how other companies or larger corporations interview and hire employees. Make some phone calls and ask some questions— you may come across some valuable information.

So, let's take a closer look.

he Bare Necessities

Who should be included in the interview process?

You may be part of an organization where either everyone wants to be involved in the interviews or no one wants to be involved. Either way, this is quite an important consideration. As usual, when dealing with any kind of human resource functions there are a couple of general rules to follow.

 Never conduct interviews with only one representative from the company present.

There are several reasons to always have more than one interviewer present. Foremost, more than one interviewer means more than one perspective. Different people look for and notice different things, and that is a definite bonus when hiring a new employee. For example, some people are more concerned with concrete mechanical questions such as technical experience or problem solving. Other interviewers are more in tune with skills or abilities that revolve around people, emotions, and compatibility. Now, all of these qualities are important in an employee and should be noted and expanded upon in an interview.

What is the best way to do that? Have more than one interviewer, each with differing opinions, ideas, and agendas regarding priorities in an employee.

 People need responsibility. They resist assuming it, but they cannot get along without it.

John Steinbeck

Additionally, interviewing well is a skill, a learned ability, and one that takes practice. Some people are, quite simply, poor interviewers. Therefore, having more than one management person in an interview increases the odds that one of them will be, if not extremely skilled, at least comfortable with the interview process.

 It is not unusual for individuals in management positions to be uncomfortable with interviewing. Do not be embarrassed if you feel less than qualified.

You must also consider that there is more than one person with a stake in hiring a new employee. In other words, the new hire will work with more than one person and be a part of what may be a much larger team. As a result, you would do well to include more than one person who will work with the new employee.

Consider:

- The new hire will have to report to a supervisor with a specific personality and management style.

- He or she may have to deal directly with customers and therefore have to interact closely with a customer-service manager.

- The person may be hired for a management position where he or she must interact in a productive manner with an entire management team or board of directors.

Whatever the case, inevitably there is more than one person in the company who is interested in or has a stake in your new employee.

What is the point of all of this?

There must be more than one person involved in the interview process. So, who should those people be?

- The applicant. (Yes, it is always a good idea for the applicant to be in the room!)

 If you work in a strictly unionized environment, there may be much stricter guidelines with respect to who and how many people must be in the interview.

- A facilitator. The facilitator is the project leader. Ideally coming from the human resources department (this certainly depends on the size of your company), the facilitator coordinates all aspects of the interview process: before, during, and after. This means from scheduling, to ensuring interviewers have copies of the candidates' resumes, to keeping the interviews running on time, to preparing the letter of offer, the facilitator leads the team.

 If your company does not have a human resources department, anyone on the hiring team may be assigned the facilitator role. Be sure to assign it to someone!

- A hiring manager. The hiring manager is the supervisor or direct manager of the new employee. Obviously this person has a huge stake in the quality of the new hire and must be included in the selection process.

- Key relationships. A key relationship is a manager or department head with whom the new employee will work closely when getting the job done. It is a good idea, if possible, to have two key relationships on the interview panel to ensure diverse perspectives on the interview team.

Including these key relationship people on the interview panel is also a nice way to ensure they have a stake in the new employee's future. In other words, by being included in the interviewing and hiring process, they are accepting shared responsibility for the person they agree should be hired. With this in mind, these key relationship people will more than likely take an interest in the continued success of this person in the company.

If you have enlisted the services of an employment agency, you may also request a representative of the agency in the interview.

Remember, hiring is a project in itself, a very important one at that, and should be treated as such. It must be organized and facilitated from beginning to end with all the players informed of the process along the way.

How many candidates will be interviewed?

Certainly there are at least two relevant factors that contribute to this question: How many resumes and applicants did you receive for the position? How many of those applicants had relevant skills, experience, and education?

You may not receive any applications with the exact qualifications you want. Decide in advance, if possible, what combination of skills, experience, and education you are willing to accept.

Ideally you will interview the top three candidates who apply. Remember, interviewing well takes time, and time for you and your interview team of management personnel means money. You must narrow the field as much as possible *before* you get to the interview stage.

Interviewing three top candidates is a fairly standard number for most companies. Not only does this keep the time commitment to a manageable level, it still offers some choice.

It could happen (hopefully not) that none of the candidates you thought were in the top three are suitable for your company. If this happens you will have to move down your list accordingly or, in the worst case, run your ad again.

How many interviews will candidates be required to pass through?

Be certain to include, right from the beginning of the interview process, all those in management who must approve the new hire. Again, it costs time and money to interview and it is pointless, inconvenient, and inconsiderate to have a candidate come back again and again to see different managers who need to approve a new employee.

In addition to being a waste of time, energy, and money, bringing candidates back again and again gives the potential employee a poor impression of your company. By repeatedly bringing a candidate back for additional interviews, your organization presents itself as confused, disorganized, and obviously unsure of its needs and priorities. Any candidate with an abundance of skills and experience to offer would think twice about working for such an organization!

It costs more money to bring an employee back several times than to interview him or her once with everyone who needs to be present!

Hiring, training, and keeping quality employees is the key to the success of your organization. Remember this and be certain all those involved in the hiring process remember it as well. With this thought in mind, it is abundantly clear that making the time to interview and hire quality people is a very real priority for all managers in your company.

Isn't it unfair and intimidating to the candidate to have too many people in the room during the interview?

Nonsense. It makes no difference how many people are in the room when you are interviewing a candidate. What does make a difference is your attitude and the attitude of the other interviewers.

It doesn't benefit you or the potential employee if you attempt to intimidate him or her during an interview. On the contrary, the more relaxed you can make a candidate during the interview, the more honest, open, and telling the interview will be.

What a man thinks of himself, that it is which determines, or rather indicates, his fate.

Henry David Thoreau

At all costs, avoid old-style intimidation tactics. This means doing away with "observers" whose only purpose is to sit and stare at the candidate during the interview. It also means adopting a warm, friendly, open, yet professional, tone and style during the interview, not a cold, stern, and humorless one. Remember, this is an honest exchange of information to benefit *both* employer and interview candidate, not an inquisition. Nowhere is it written that everyone who participates should be nervous and uncomfortable or the interview is a failure!

Should peers be involved in the interview?

No. That was a quick answer wasn't it? Consider these four major risks.

A "peer" is an individual already working for your company who is at the same level and will be working with the new employee you hire.

Risk 1. Although you may be tempted to enlist the assistance of employees in the hiring process under the guise that they will be most closely associated with the new employee and therefore should be involved, resist the urge. If you are considering it, remember that once you extend the privilege to employees, it will be extremely difficult to revoke—even if it doesn't work to the benefit of your organization. Employees may become adamant about being involved in all hiring decisions and become annoyed when they are not included.

Risk 2. You run the risk of individuals being hired to be part of a team simply because "we like them," not because their skills are appropriately suited to the group. (Conversely, an individual who would nicely complement the team may not be hired by a peer because of some personal differences, or perhaps an interviewing peer has a friend applying for the position whom he or she would rather hire.) Certainly a new employee must be liked by the rest of the team and must fit with the organization, but that should not be the only criterion for being hired.

 A good way to encourage employee participation in the hire is to ask for input in the needs analysis stage. Ask peers what skills and qualities they feel are essential for the new hire to possess.

Risk 3. As has been mentioned on several occasions, hiring a new employee is a costly venture from the interview process through to the training. With that in mind, you must consider that employees involved in the hiring process will not be prepared to accept the responsibility of a poor hire. Peers will not be involved in any of the additional training that may be necessary, or the follow-up performance reviews, or the meetings attempting to redirect a new employee who is not working out well.

Risk 4. Ask yourself if employee peers would be willing to accept any legal challenges should they arise during any stage of the interviewing or hiring procedure. Chances are the answer to that question is no. Therefore, with these things in mind, hiring should remain a management right and a management responsibility, period. There is far too much riding on making a sound hiring decision to make it a decision of emotional hit and miss.

Where will the interviews be held?

This may seem like a trivial question, and the first answer that pops into your head may be "wherever, what does it matter?" Well, although it isn't a life-and-death problem, it is something to be considered.

There are a number of people participating in the interview, and chances are you will not all fit into one person's office. Even if you can cram into one office it would, no doubt, be hot and eventually unbearable. Use a conference room of some kind, and if you do not have a conference room book a hotel room.

 Never is there either work without reward nor reward without work being expended.

Livy

Why?

Not only is the interview designed for candidates to "sell" themselves to you, it is also a forum for you, as an organization, to "sell" yourself to the appropriate candidate. It would be a little difficult to convince a hardworking, go-getter of an employee that you are on the cutting edge of your industry when you interview him or her in the back storage room!

Additionally, although a gourmet sushi buffet is not required for the interviewers and the interviewees, it is a good idea to have water and coffee available. Each interview may last over an hour, so a beverage of some kind for the people participating is necessary.

Booking appropriate space and having beverages on hand are some of the responsibilities of the interview facilitator.

How should interviews be scheduled?

Hopefully you have been able to find a day when all the managers involved in the interviews are available to interview.

Do not hesitate to remind managers that nothing is more important than recruiting quality staff for the well-being of your organization!

Once you have your day in mind (and your space) it should be fairly easy to schedule meetings. By this time you have also narrowed your candidate field to a nice manageable number. Remember, three interviews in one day, for one position, is ideal. If you try to do more, you will quickly understand why the standard number is three candidates. Any more than that and not only do the interviewers begin to tire of asking the same questions over and over again, but they begin to think that all the answers sound suspiciously the same and also that they are falling behind in their other duties. Indeed, more than three interviews in one day is unfair to both interviewers and candidates.

You can lead a horse to water, but you can't make him drink it.

Unknown

If this is your first time coordinating interviews for your company, it is easy to become overzealous and want to interview as many people as possible. This is a natural inclination since it is difficult to narrow the field simply by looking at resumes and speaking with people over the phone. You feel you must meet people in person to make a good decision. Once again, resist the temptation to interview more than three people. In the end you will find you're not able to do a good job of interviewing, and all your good intentions will be lost.

How long should each interview be?

Now that we have the numbers agreed upon, what about the time frame? Well, here is a general outline.

Plan for an hour-and-a-half per interview whether you think you will use it or not. Be sure to schedule at least twenty minutes between interviews if they are back-to-back to give your interview panel time to discuss the last candidate and to grab a coffee or take a bathroom break.

 If you find after twenty minutes of interviewing, for whatever reason, the candidate is completely unsuited to your organization, do not be afraid to thank the person for his or her time and end the interview. You don't want to waste your time or the candidate's. Make sure you have a previously agreed-upon signal to confirm with the other interviewers that you all have the same intention.

If possible, have all interviews scheduled for one day. This way the interviewers are in the right frame of mind, and all the candidates are fresh in everyone's mind. If possible, begin the interviews first thing in the morning. For example, start a half hour after the office opens to ensure everyone is energetic, but still giving them time to get there, return any important calls, or do any last-minute rescheduling. Be sure to take a lunch break!

After the final interview of the day, in addition to the time after each interview, have some time set aside to once again go over each interviewer's notes and thoughts on the candidates. Perhaps your company has a scoring system in place for interviews; now is the time to review it more extensively.

Certainly as you become more experienced as an interviewer and as your company continues to hire employees you will become more adept at the process. Along the way you will, no doubt, develop a system that works best for you, the rest of the management team, and your organization.

The Finer Details

You have the basics but there are still some unanswered questions about interviewing. (As a matter of fact, you probably have some questions about interview questions specifically!) So, let's get down to the heart of the matter.

Before you begin, as bureaucratic as it sounds, someone must be in charge of the interview.

Why?

Well, it is important that someone control the movement of the interview, the timing, and the coordinating of the candidate (for lack of a better term). Granted, interviews are scheduled, you know who will participate, and who will be interviewed. What more coordination need there be?

Well, just the little bits, frankly. A person has already been designated the facilitator, and for convenience sake, it is presumably the same person who has screened resumes and scheduled interviews, although this is not necessarily so. So what more is he or she expected to do?

Well, one person should be responsible for greeting the candidate at the front entrance or reception area. That same person should also introduce the candidate to all parties in the interview process. All the interviewers should be introduced by first and last name and their position, and how they "fit in" with the whole process should be indicated.

This person will probably be the one to initiate the interview process, facilitating the movement of conversation from small talk and introductions to the actual interview proper.

The interview proper is the "main course," the "meat and potatoes" of the interview.

Additionally, this individual is to be responsible for ensuring each interviewer has a "package" on each candidate. This means a copy of the appropriate resume, cover letter, etc., a copy of the job description, and a list of the questions each candidate is to be asked.

During the interview process, the facilitator will also be the one to gauge the progress of the interview and the reactions of the other interviewers. For example, it may happen that shortly after the start of the interview it becomes clear to all parties present that, for whatever reason, this candidate is inappropriate for your company or for the position. It is the facilitator's responsibility to assess the thoughts of the other interviewers, probably by some prearranged signal, and end the interview early if deemed necessary.

The signal to the facilitator to end the interview may be as simple as a shift in the direction of a pen on the desk in front of each of the interviewers.

Finally, at the close of each interview it is imperative the interview panel discuss their impressions of each candidate while the interview is fresh in their minds. It is the role of the facilitator to orchestrate this exchange of opinions and information. This may be an informal discussion, or it may be discussion of a company rating system each candidate is evaluated by.

Be sure to decide ahead of time how the discussion following each interview should go. This is an essential portion of the interview and must be completed within specific time restraints. Everyone must know what is expected of him or her.

Certainly it sounds like an awful lot of work for the facilitator on interview day, but really, the facilitator's job is simply to ensure everything runs smoothly for interviewers and candidates alike. Remember, the fewer glitches there are during the day, the more time there is for important information exchange.

So, at this point, there really is nothing more to think about than how to get the interview going, what questions to ask, and who should ask them.

Getting the Interview Going

You may be thinking to yourself, "getting what going—the candidate walks in, sits down, you start interviewing, right?"

OK, it's something like that.

You, as an interviewer and as a manager of an organization, have a few responsibilities to any candidate you choose to interview. It is in your best interest to make sure every individual who is interviewed for a position with your company is comfortable in your space and with the group of interviewers. Again, it does nothing for you, for the candidate, or for your goal as an interviewer to intimidate the people you propose to interview.

There is no verbal vitamin more potent than praise.

Frederick B. Harris

Second, you need to be certain each interviewee knows exactly what is expected of him or her should he or she be hired. Again, it is in your best interest to do this at the outset of the interview so everyone knows exactly where he or she stands. How do you do this?

After you have introduced everyone in the room begin by describing your company and what it is you do, and perhaps where it is your organization wants to go. (From this, the interview candidate knows immediately whether his or her plans for the future fit with the goals of your company.)

Presumably, prior to these first formal steps there has been some small talk as you were entering the interview room and settling—whether it be about the weather, the drive in, current events, or whatever. It is human nature, for the most part, to chat with someone you have just introduced yourself to—don't fight it!

Follow your company outline with a thorough description of the position and how it fits within the company. (Again, now the candidate knows what is expected in this position, where he or she would fit as part of the team if hired, and if he or she is still interested in the position.)

Remember, not only are you interviewing these individuals, they are interviewing you and your organization. If they have some marketable skills, which presumably they do since you wanted to interview them, and some solid experience, they may also have some additional irons in the fire. In other words, do not assume that because someone is at an interview with your organization he or she is automatically going to jump at any offer you present.

As mentioned earlier, employees with valuable skills and experience can be choosy in today's starved market, and you as an employer need to make yourself attractive.

Now, you may also choose to inform each candidate at the beginning of the interview how many other people are being interviewed, when interviews will be completed, if there will be a second interview, and when a decision about who will be hired will be made. You may, however, choose to omit this information completely and leave it up to the candidate to ask if he or she is interested. It's your choice.

After you have given an overview of the company and position, invite the candidate to ask any further questions he or she may have.

As a final note, while you are still settling into the interview and making the transition from setting the tone and making the candidate comfortable to the formal interview, many interviewers will ask candidates to talk a little bit about themselves: "So, why don't you begin by telling us a bit about yourself?"

Now, this question is normally asked with the best of intentions, but if you have ever been on the receiving end of it, it is a hateful question.

 Information's pretty thin stuff unless mixed with experience.

Clarence Day

Most interviewees wonder what it is you want to know specifically: do you want to know about them personally or professionally, do you want a short answer or a long one, is there a hidden meaning to this question that remains to be discovered, or are you, as an interviewer, just being cruel! You get the idea.

So, although it can be a great question for you in as much as you get to know a bit about the candidate, his or her likes and dislikes, maybe things you have in common, know that it is often stressful for the interviewee. To help alleviate the stress, try to be specific when you ask the question.

 Remember, it is in the interest of both parties for the interview candidate to be relaxed.

For example, "Chris, we'd like you to be relaxed, and we'd like to get to know you better, so why don't you begin by telling us what you like to do in your spare time" lets the candidate know exactly what the question is for and what you would like to hear. Any information you want to gather about the candidate's work history will be touched on later, and you should have very specific questions prepared for that purpose.

 If you have a better question with the same purpose in mind, I would love to hear it and so would thousands of interview candidates out there!

Don't be afraid to go off on a tangent or two during this question. If Chris mentions snowboarding as a great passion and you are a beginner, don't be afraid to ask for a few pointers on where to buy a board. It gets the interview off to a great start!

So, with the completion of that question, and any brief resulting discussion, you are ready to begin the information-gathering portion of the interview.

 Arrange interview seating to be comfortable and intimate, not inquisition-like. Do not have the candidate backed into a corner or seated in a chair that makes him or her sit lower than everyone else. Remember, this is a dialogue between professionals with both sides wanting to gain.

As information gathering is the key issue of any interview, it is important to ask the right questions.

What Questions Are Best?

Although every interview is different because every company and every candidate is different, there are fundamentally two types of questions to be asked during an interview: fact-finding or concrete questions, for example, "How many years of customer-service experience do you have?" and behavioral or descriptive questions, for example, "Describe an occasion when you had a disagreement of some type with a coworker. How did you resolve it, and would you do anything different if you could do it again?"

Obviously, fact-finding questions are very straightforward and give you solid information about technical skills, education, years of experience, and that sort of thing. These questions can often be answered by a simple answer or even a yes or no. If a question can, in fact, be answered by a yes or no, it is called a closed-ended question.

Closed-ended questions are necessary, but be sure not to overuse them. From an interviewer's perspective they are easy for the interview candidate to answer but offer little insight into the candidate's personality.

You can nicely turn what could be a closed-ended question into an open one, however, simply by asking the candidate to give an example. For example, to "Do you consider yourself a skilled problem solver?" now add, "Please give an example of how you effectively solved a problem."

To "Is your career where you expected it to be at this point?" now add, "Why or why not?"

To "Do you consider yourself a quick learner?" now add, "Can you give us an example where you had to assimilate new information very quickly?"

You get the idea. Remember, the more information you can get now, the better. You will, of course, find some interview candidates naturally use examples to illustrate their experience and others do not. Granted, it is a little more work for you when they don't, but it is still to your benefit to work at making the candidates expand on their answers wherever possible.

 Our chief want in life is somebody who will make us do what we can.

Ralph Waldo Emerson

Behavioral or descriptive questions are designed specifically to be open ended so the interview candidate is required to explain, describe, and give examples. These questions may encompass their philosophy on work, their behavior in the work environment, or specific examples of everything from problem solving to determining priorities.

The theory behind these types of questions, in a nutshell, is that past behavior predicts future performance. In other words, you can gain considerable insight into how interviewees will behave if hired by your organization based on how they have managed themselves in their previous work environments. These types of questions can be very interesting for you, as an employer, and you should take full advantage of them.

Design questions, for example, that describe a particular scenario to the interviewees, one that would occur in the position you are interviewing for, and ask them to illustrate how they would manage the situation. You may ask them to include examples from their past which further illustrate the skills they would use in solving this particular problem, or you may leave it up to them whether they choose to use examples at all. Either way, you know how you, as an employer, would want the problem or situation resolved and you quickly come to know if the candidate subscribes to that same philosophy.

 For any long-term employer/employee working relationship, it is imperative you have at least a similar working philosophy.

Here are some examples:

- "It's four o'clock Friday afternoon and your computer crashes, taking with it a presentation for first thing Monday. What do you do?"

- "You discover a coworker stealing company property. What do you do?"

- "If chosen for this position, how will you go about familiarizing yourself with our policies, procedures, and the other employees?"

- "A coworker continually puts you down and embarrasses you in front of other staff. What do you do?"

You can see where these questions are going. Although there are some facts to be gathered, they are more interested in uncovering a potential employee's personality, work philosophy, and communication skills. You'll also notice the answers to these questions have the potential to be quite time consuming—plan your interview accordingly.

 Please note these questions are not specifically designed for your organization, but are more geared toward discovering a candidate's work ethic. Be certain to ask questions illustrating conditions that exist specifically in your workplace.

If an interview is going well, there should be no shortage of questions you want to ask, and each answer the candidate gives will often lead naturally to another question. Be certain you don't get carried away with the conversational nature of some interviews and forget to ask all the questions you intended to. It is important you ask all three interview candidates fundamentally the same questions in order to effectively compare them. Be sure each interviewer has a list and they refer to it frequently.

Don't try to "wing it" in an interview. Have specific questions which are prepared in advance and agreed upon by all interviewers.

The other way to ensure you ask for all the information you require to make an informed hiring decision is to assign specific questions to each interviewer.

Assigning Questions

So you have your list of questions which you and the other interviewers discussed and agreed upon prior to the interview. No doubt you have a variety of questions in a variety of forms which will give you a broad range of information about each candidate. Who should ask which questions, and does it matter?

Well, there are a couple of reasons to assign specific questions to specific interviewers.

What?

Some interviewers are naturally more chatty than others, and by assigning questions you ensure all interviewers participate. You may ask yourself what does it matter if everyone talks during the interview. Well, it keeps everyone interested and participating throughout the interview, it ensures each of the interviewers feel as though he or she has a direct opinion and/or stake in the hiring of a new employee (this certainly comes into greater play when orientation and training begins), and it also gives a nice indication of how the interview candidate responds to different management types and their differing styles.

Have the facilitator organize the list of questions so each interviewer is clear about which questions he or she is to ask. Have extra copies on hand.

Now that you agree it is important that everyone participate, does it matter who asks which questions? Not really. Perhaps the main deciding factor is personal interest for the interviewer. For example, the customer-service manager certainly is interested in how this potential employee handles himself or herself with clients, so he or she may choose to ask questions directly related to communication and interpersonal skills. On the other hand, the manager may want someone else to ask those questions so he or she may listen more effectively and take some notes.

Each interviewer may have some questions he or she wants to ask, but as facilitator, you will probably have to suggest additional questions to round out the interview.

As a quick aside at this point, although you've divided the questions so everyone asks some, organize it in such a way that there is still a logical progression to the interview. For example, group all the education questions together, then the work-experience questions, followed by the candidate's goals for the future, and so on. Grouping topics of discussion keeps the interview more coherent in general, makes it easier for you to keep track of what has and has not been asked, and facilitates and encourages deeper probing into issues because you stay on one topic for the duration of a few questions. Additionally, it makes it easier for the candidate to focus his or her thoughts to particular time frames in his or her work history, for instance, and you will receive more information in a more comprehensive manner.

As you are starting to see, interview "preproduction" is essential. You must take the time prior to any interviewing to discuss with the interview team the course of action. One such issue to discuss is note taking. Some human-resource professionals suggest everyone take notes so you may compare after the interview, others suggest only one person take notes so everyone else is focused on the candidate.

 Remember to schedule enough time between interviews to discuss any notes that were taken.

My suggestion is for everyone to jot things down, on a separate piece of paper—not on the candidate's resume—whenever something piques their interest. Each interviewer may not have copious notes on every question, but even a quick note on your impression of an answer will facilitate discussion at the end of each interview and therefore the decision-making process after all interviews.

Are you having fun yet?! Yes, this is a lot of work and there are a lot of things to consider, but as the saying goes, the more you put into it, the more you get out of it! Persevere, you'll be glad you did and it will be easier next time.

The Beginning of the End— Reference Checks

Presumably at this stage you have completed your interviews, you have discussed the various candidates with the other interviewers, and you have a good idea of which candidate you are considering hiring.

Now what?

Before each candidate leaves the interview office, have him or her leave references for you to call. If, for whatever reason, a candidate does not have a list of references with him or her at the interview, have the candidate fax them to you by the end of that business day. Reference checks are an integral part of the interview process, and the candidates must realize that the interview is not complete until you have thoroughly checked references.

Be sure to have a quick look at the references the interview candidate gives you while he or she is still in your presence.

Why?

You must have business or past employer work references to check, and a list of all personal references is simply not adequate. If you find a candidate has given you only personal references, or references that will prove impossible to contact, insist he or she fax you more appropriate ones by the close of the business day.

 Try to do your reference checks soon after the interviews while all the information is fresh in your mind.

Now, business references do not necessarily have to be paid employment. For example, volunteer work is still work done in a business environment, under the supervision or direction of an "employer." Now, granted, that "employer" may be the parents of the members of the local minor hockey team, but your interview candidate was still accountable to those parents to deliver a satisfactory product.

References do not always have to be past employers, either. The reference could be:

- a peer from the office

- a volunteer who worked with or for your candidate

- a manager in the workplace

- a customer who dealt routinely with your candidate

- or perhaps one of those parents whose child played on that hockey team

All of these are professional relationships and are good sources of information for you as a potential employer. Be certain you get the references you want, not just whoever the candidate happens to have on his or her list.

So now that you have the list, what do you do with it? There are those employers who feel references are really not that important to check, that they can get all the information they need from their interview with the candidate. Now let's think about that for a minute. You have spent an hour with this person gathering information around certain questions and answers. You have the opportunity to extend that information resource to speaking with someone who may have worked with this person for years. Who do you think will have more insight into this potential employee's work habits and ethics? Call the references, and plan to spend some time doing it.

If there is any hesitation about whether or not you want to check references, think about all the time, effort, and money this interview process has cost your organization. If one more step can help you be that much more certain you are hiring the right individual, isn't it worth taking?

You may ask yourself at the outset of checking references if you are really going to get honest information from these people. We all know someone who was desperate for a work reference so they used their Aunt Mary's name who is the vice president of marketing at the company they worked at for two weeks one summer. Fortunately, Aunt Mary has a different last name, and who bothers to check references anyway! Well, if that was then, this is now—employers check references. Frankly, if there is dirt to be found on a potential employee, a thorough reference check will find it.

He who stands on tiptoe does not stand firm; he who takes the longest strides is not the fastest walker; he who boasts of what he will do seldom succeeds in all he promises.

Chinese Proverb

So, how do you go about doing an effective reference check? First of all, plan to spend at least half an hour on the phone with each reference. Obviously, if you are planning to spend that kind of time on the phone with someone, you must be up front with him or her at the beginning of the conversation. Explain who you are, explain why you are calling, mention how long you expect this interview to take, and determine a convenient time to call back if now is a bad time.

Basically a good reference check revisits all the information you gathered during the interview of the *top two* candidates only. This is going to take some time and it will be worth it to you to do a good job, but you don't want to have to do it for more than two people.

Knowledge rests not upon truth alone, but upon error also.

C. G. Jung

So what do you ask?

The idea of the reference check right off the top is to confirm the information you were given by the candidate.

- Did the person really work there?

- Were his or her responsibilities what he or she said they were?

- Did the person come to work consistently or was attendance a problem?

- Would this employer hire the candidate again given the opportunity?

In addition, you will want to ask some questions that relate specifically to your work environment. For example, after giving the reference a brief job description outlining the major physical, clerical, and/or administrative duties the job would entail, ask where he or she feels the candidate would be most challenged and why.

Perhaps you will need to ask specific scenario questions such as, "There are a lot of gossipers in the office. How do you feel Chris would operate in that type of environment?"

Another good question is, "Was there anything that prevented Chris from coming to work or doing the job?"

Once again, other than confirming information you received in the interview, these are the type of questions you will want to put to references. Ultimately, be prepared to take a long time to check the references of your top two candidates and do it well. A good reference check will pay off in the long run.

Top Ten Reasons NOT to Hire Someone

1. He insists his mother must meet you before he can accept the job.

2. For the life of her, she can't remember the name of your company.

3. He assures you his grandmother will give an excellent character reference . . . but remember to speak up.

4. She asks if you have any objections to her taking her pet snake along on sales calls.

5. In the interview, you ask him to tell you about himself, and he says no.

6. Her cellular phone rings during the interview . . . and she answers it!

7. He tells you "I left my last job because I got bored, so I just quit going."

8. You show her where her new office would be, and she asks if hanging a "Do Not Disturb" sign on the door would be a problem.

9. You ask if he has any questions for you and he says, "huh?"

10. Her idea of illustrating a point with an example in the interview is to add, "and I did it good," to her yes or no answer.

The closest to perfection a person
ever comes is when he fills out a job
application form.

Stanley J. Randall

Chapter 4

They Came, You Interviewed, You Hired

When you get right down to the root
of the meaning of the word
succeed, you find that it simply
means to follow through.

F. W. Nichol

You did all the work, and there was a lot of work to be done! You compared notes, you checked references, you rechecked your notes, and somewhere in there your instincts kicked in and helped, and you made a decision. You hired someone, perhaps not the person you "liked" the most, but the person you knew was most suitable for your company and its goals.

So now you have a few phone calls to make. As a courtesy to the candidates you interviewed and did not choose, you must call them and thank them for their time and explain you will keep their resumes on file. During these phone calls, expect the candidates who were not chosen to want to know why they were not selected. It is part of your job to give them some honest feedback.

Be sure to schedule enough time to do this. It is an important conclusion to the interview process and deserves to be treated as such.

If you work in human resources and the candidate you have interviewed was an internal candidate (someone who already works for the organization), then it is your responsibility to give feedback on their interview style. Still, this should be done in a candid yet tactful manner. For example, "Let's talk about your interview and some things you might like to think about for next time." Or, "Now that you have gone through this style of interview and are more familiar with behavioral-style questioning, how could you be more prepared for the next time?"

If the candidate is not an internal one, then your responsibility to give feedback is certainly more precarious. As an employer, you would do well to focus on the skills of the candidate you did hire. For example, "The candidate we chose had five years of administrative experience, which we felt would fit with our long-term goals. Additionally, although your skills are excellent, the candidate we selected had computer skills more suited to our immediate needs." That sort of thing. Indeed, it is safer and, as an employer, more prudent to stick to commenting on technical job requirements when giving feedback to candidates who were not hired.

However the phone call goes, be straightforward, yet prudent. Not only will this help the individual in future interviews, it will keep the door open for you should you have additional hiring needs in the future.

 There is the possibility the person you hired will not work out, so it is in your best interest to end your relationship with the "runner-up" candidates on a positive note.

Granted, these may be awkward phone calls, but take a deep breath and do the best job you can. Think of it as your obligation to the betterment of the business community!

Now the uncomfortable work is complete, and you've nicely and professionally tied up the loose ends. It is time to focus on your new employee.

Getting Past "You're Hired"

Although it would be great if all you had to do was invite the new hire to work with you and that would be the end of it, unfortunately it doesn't work that way. There will be quite an adjustment period, a different one for every individual, while the new employee gets comfortable with your company. The question you need to ask is "What can I do to facilitate a quick settling-in period?" Knowing that the sooner your new employee is comfortable, the sooner everyone will be more productive, it is in your best interest and that of the company to work hard at your new employee orientation.

What?

Well, getting right down to it, one of the first things on your new employee "to do" list is the official letter of offer. Presumably you have offered the position to one of the interview candidates and he or she has accepted. Now it's time to make it official and put it in writing. How?

 This letter may be an important document to refer to at a later date should there be discrepancies over hiring details.

The letter of offer should include:

- the salary agreed upon for the position

- the probationary period or term (probably three months)

- the confidentiality clause if it pertains to your business (this states that the work the employee does for your company is confidential, and the employee is legally bound to maintain the confidential nature of that work)

- the specifics of any benefits the employee is entitled to

- any additional compensation (this may include commissions or variable pay)

- any entitlements you agreed upon (this may include a car, clothing or moving allowance, etc.)

Have this letter completed before the employee begins work. It should be completed with a copy made for your records and for the employee's and be available to review with the new employee on his or her first day.

 There may be some negotiating of salary or benefits to be done before this letter can be completed. Whatever the details, it should be ready for the first day of employment.

The Time Line

For your new employee's first day consider yourself the appointed Welcome Wagon representative. You need to do what you can to make the new hire feel comfortable and feel that he or she is a welcome member of the team.

How?

There are a number of little things you can do to get things started on the right foot with your new associate:

- Have business cards printed and ready for the new employee when he or she arrives.

- Put up a notice on the bulletin board introducing the new member to the rest of the team.

- Ensure the new employee's computer, phone, and other office equipment are hooked up and working.

- Have the employee's work space ready for him or her to move into and personalize.

- Compile an orientation package for the new employee including information about the company, benefits, holidays, special events, an organizational chart including the names of coworkers, and any company practices that are unique to your organization.

In addition to these housekeeping issues, there are the personal touches you need to think about. This employee may be not only new to your company, he or she may be new to the city. Show him (or her) around the office, including everything from introductions to where the bathrooms are. Show him around the area, and let him know where the good restaurants are. Perhaps your new employee likes to go for walks at lunch. If so, explain where the closest park or walking track is. You get the idea.

The more pleasant an employee's initial experiences are with your organization, the more likely it is he or she will want to stay.

Another good idea is to assign your new employee a buddy. A what?! A buddy. Introduce the new employee to someone who works in his or her department, someone who has been there for a time, someone who has a positive attitude and knows the ropes. This will be the person the new employee can rely upon to help him or her acclimatize to the new office, perhaps reminding the new hire where to find the stationery or helping him or her remember everyone's name.

After the first week, sit down with the newest member of your team to discuss the more formal aspects of the orientation process. Take the time, particularly in a large organization, to discuss the culture of the organization, the company mandate, and the goals of the team. Be sure to discuss with the new employee how he or she, as a new team member, fits with the organization and its future.

The deepest principle of human nature is the craving to be appreciated.

William James

Do not do this orientation the first day. There is far too much information for the employee to try to grasp as it is, and you want to save any important information for when the initial shock wears off. After the first week, a new hire will have a clearer notion of the company and where he or she fits in, and you can simply fill in the blanks or expand the picture accordingly.

In the Thick of It

After your initial meeting and orientation with your new employee, it is important to schedule follow-up evaluations. These initial meetings are certainly for your benefit and for the new employee's. These performance meetings give you a chance to address any concerns you have regarding the employee's progress and productivity and to redirect or refocus them if necessary. Additionally, this is a time for the employee to mention any problems he or she may be having or make any suggestions that would help make him or her a more beneficial member of the team.

Make it clear to the new employee to approach his or her supervisor directly if there is a problem, but mention there will be a formal meeting within three months.

If you do not feel there are any issues that need to be addressed, it is fine to schedule this initial check-in for three months from the initial employment start date. If, on the other hand, you feel the employee does require some redirection, it is in your interest to schedule a monthly meeting until things are on track. Normally, after three months you will have a very good idea whether or not you have a successful match of your new employee and your organization.

Only dead fish swim with the stream.

Unknown

If you are finding things aren't exactly what you had hoped they would be when you first hired this new employee, don't be too quick to hold him or her completely responsible. The supervisor or team leader must have some stake in the new employee as well. If you recall, when deciding who would participate in the interview process, part of the reason for including additional management was to ensure that, after an employee was chosen, the interview team would feel some responsibility toward ensuring the new person worked out.

Well, if things are seeming a little shaky with the new employee, don't forget to call on the other managers who were involved in the hiring process. Now, this is not a finger-pointing session where you all get together to decide who is to be blamed for the shortcomings in the new employee. What it is, is a time to examine where some support measures may be implemented to facilitate the success of the new team member.

Any time someone new joins your organization it is an adjustment for everyone in that organization. There will be changes whether this is a completely new position or the new employee is replacing someone who left.

 If the new employee is filling an existing position, remember he or she is new. This means new methods and new ideas, and things will be different than they were. Embrace the change.

Although the new employee may have a buddy to ease the transition, it is necessary to prepare management, especially the direct supervisor, for the transition as well. It will have to be made clear to the supervisor that there will be a considerable time commitment for him or her while the employee adapts to the intricacies of your organization.

This may mean brief meetings to check in and see how things are progressing. It may mean the supervisor will have to closely watch the end product of the new employee to ensure it meets company standards. It may mean assisting, if necessary, in the resolution of any initial personality conflicts among the new team before difficulties arise. Or it may mean recommending and implementing some additional training for the new staff member to bring him or her up to a standard skill level. Once again, it is not only the responsibility of the new employee to work at fitting in. This is a team venture and must be treated as such.

No doubt, before you hire someone, you will have an idea of how much additional training he or she will need. Always expect (and be prepared) to have to do more rather than less.

Investing in Your Employees

By now you and your new employee have decided that you have a match, and this relationship is working well for you both. You are happy with the progress of the new hire and the potential he or she exhibits; and he or she is pleased with the working environment and the compensation for his or her efforts. So, how do you keep this relationship growing and developing so you don't have to go through the hiring procedure again any time soon? Training.

Training is the ultimate investment in your employees, and in today's business market, an essential one as well. By training your employees, not only do you keep them productive, current, competitive, and happy, you also automatically create a built-in promotional ladder for your organization. In other words, the more time, effort, and money you spend training your existing employees, the less likely you are to have to hire skilled workers and management from outside the company or to need to bring in contract employees. It is much easier for you as a manager to promote from within your organization than to have to go through the entire hiring process. By continually training your employees, you ensure you will have quality people within the organization to promote and to help move the company in the direction you want it to go.

Training may mean in-house seminars, formal classroom education, weekend workshops, night classes, or any combination of these.

Now, before you get that notion in your head and run with the idea that you will simply train all your employees and that they will progress nicely up the corporate ladder, and in the future you will only have to hire entry-level employees, consider this: just because you are a star quarterback doesn't automatically make you a great coach. Or alternately, you don't have to be a star quarterback to be an outstanding coach.

This means that not everyone is interested in the corporate ladder, not everyone wants to move up that ladder, and not everyone, even if they are interested in it, will be ladder-climbing material. You, as a manager, must be adept in the art of skill recognition.

 The trouble with using experience as a guide is that the final exam often comes first and then the lesson.

Unknown

What?

As a manager, it is essential that you either work closely enough with your employees, or you have excellent communication with their supervisors, so that you are constantly aware of their progress and their desire for progress. Presumably, this constant awareness will also give you a very good idea of what type of skills each of your employees excels at. Are they technical people, do they have excellent communication skills, do they work well with others? All of these observations on your part will give insight into whether your employees are destined to be coaches or whether they would most benefit the company continuing as starting quarterbacks.

It is common for managers to assume that because an employee has exceptional hard skills (technical or trade skills) that he or she also will automatically have superior soft skills (people and communication skills) to go along with them, thus making him or her excellent management material. This is not always the case. As a matter of fact, it is rarely the case.

Be extremely careful not to judge employees too quickly or to not allow for change. Remember, it is always to your advantage for employees to grow in your organization—be open to it.

What all of this means to you, as a manager, is that although it is to your benefit and your company's benefit to promote from within, you must realize that not everyone wants or has the skills to move into positions of greater breadth and responsibility. You must hone your ability to recognize those employees with the skills, potential, and desire to move up the corporate ladder.

As you develop your hiring skills you will be better prepared to assess what kind of potential an employee has. Add to this the knowledge you have of your company with respect to what it needs now and in the future, and you can nicely begin to prepare for the long term. Make it a point to keep your organization, its strengths and weaknesses, and its needs for the future in the front of your mind as you go through the hiring process. Remember, you are hiring for your immediate needs and for the future.

 Just as some people are natural managers, some people have excellent hiring instincts. Try to be objective about your skills as a hiring manager. Perhaps you are a natural, or perhaps, if the option is there, you would do well to organize and facilitate but have someone else interview and hire.

Ultimately, for your company to be successful and for your employees, new and old, to be successful you must be willing to support them.

If you empower your employees and offer open lines of communication to management, fair compensation, and regular training to ensure their competitive edge, not only will you have to hire less frequently, you will find it much easier to attract quality employees.

Remember, as in all things you must offer and be quality to attract quality. What kind of organization is yours?

After the Smoke Clears

Well, you may feel as though a bomb has gone off in your office, but you do have a new employee to show for your efforts. Well, actually, you have a whole lot more than that.

What?

You have a well-researched, comprehensive needs analysis which has given you a much greater understanding of your organization, its future, and its staffing.

You also have a well-defined job description (which of course is continually evolving, but the foundation is more than complete).

Most importantly, however, you have a new understanding, and no doubt new respect, for the hiring process. You set out to do it because it was necessary, you worked through the groundwork, you recruited the assistance of your fellow managers (who learned some things as well), and, frankly, you did it!

The face of business is changing and with it so are the skills you as a manager, executive, or owner of your own business must have. Hiring well isn't *exactly* an easy process (this book is only slightly misnamed!). And now having done it, you have added a considerable skill to your resume, making you, and therefore your organization, that much more competitive.

Well done.

The difference between the impossible and the possible lies in a person's determination.

Tommy Lasorda

Conclusion

Hiring Made Easy. Well, it probably wasn't the easiest thing you have ever done in your life, and it was a bit time-consuming, but it was well worth the effort and the education. You have a new employee and some new skills to show for it.

As the face of business changes, so too does the face of hiring. But—no matter how you look at it—you, as an employer, are always looking for quality employees to stay with your organization and help you build it. Hiring that kind of employee will always take time and effort, no matter how much business and technology change.

You persevered, however, and I trust you found a quality person to work with you. You rethought and readjusted your goals and ideals surrounding your business and that has helped you provide a more focused, quality organization for your new employee to grow within.

You are building a team destined for success!

WARNER MEMORIAL LIBRARY
EASTERN COLLEGE
ST. DAVIDS, PA. 19087

WARNER MEMORIAL LIBRARY
EASTERN COLLEGE
ST. DAVIDS, PA. 19087